W9-AAD-890

SALADS

Cooking with Style

THUNDER BAY
P·R·E·S·S

Published by
Thunder Bay Press
5880 Oberlin Drive, Suite 400
San Diego, California 92121

Produced by Weldon Russell Pty Ltd
107 Union Street, North Sydney, NSW 2060, Australia

A member of the Weldon International Group of Companies

Copyright © 1994 Weldon Russell Pty Ltd

Publisher: Elaine Russell
Publishing manager: Susan Hurley
Author and home economist: Jane Hann
Editor: Kayte Nunn
US cooking consultant: Mardee Haidin Regan
Designer: Catherine Martin
Photographer: Rowan Fotheringham
Food stylist: Jane Hann
Production: Dianne Leddy

All rights reserved. No part of this publication may be reproduced, stored in a retrieval system, or transmitted in any form or by any means, electronic, mechanical, photocopying, recording or otherwise, without the prior written permission of Thunder Bay Press.

Library of Congress Cataloging-in-Publication data
Hann, Jane, 1955–
    Salads / [author and home economist, Jane Hann ; photographer, Rowan Fotheringham].
       p.   cm. — (Cooking with style)
    ISBN 1–57145–001–7 : $13.95
    1. Salads. I. Title. II. Series.
  TX740.H274 1994
  641.8'3—dc20   93–49609
                                        CIP

Printed by Tien Wah Press, Singapore

A KEVIN WELDON PRODUCTION

Acknowledgments: Cydonia — The Glass Studio, Sydney; Hale Imports; Royal Copenhagen; Lalique; Villeroy & Boch

Cover: *Avocado, Fennel and Orange Salad with Balsamic Vinaigrette*
Back cover: *Grilled Baby Eggplant Salad with Cumin, Coriander and Yogurt Dressing*
Opposite: *Smoked Salmon, Asparagus and Cantaloupe Salad with Red Bell Pepper Mayonnaise*
(recipe on page 96)

CONTENTS

Vegetables

Antipasto Salad Platter   44

Mixed Leaf Salad   46

Spring Vegetable Salad with Tomato and Basil Salsa Dressing   48

Warm Mixed Mushroom and Asparagus Salad   50

Grilled Baby Eggplant Salad with Cumin, Coriander and Yogurt Dressing   52

Baby Squash and Yellow Pepper Salad with Raspberry Vinaigrette   54

Broccoli Salad with Basil Vinaigrette   56

Leek and Sun-dried Tomato Salad with Mustard Vinaigrette   58

Roasted Tomato Salad   60

Green Bean Salad with Roasted Macadamia Nuts and Macadamia Nut Oil Vinaigrette   62

Herb and Potato Frittata Salad with Tomato and Onion Salsa   64

Mixed Potato Salad wih Mint Pesto Dressing   66

Pulses & Grains

Couscous Tabbouleh   68

Wild Rice Salad with Orange Vinaigrette   70

White Bean Salad with Tuna and Black Olives   72

Jasmine Rice Salad   74

Chick Pea Salad with Fresh Herb Vinaigrette   76

Cheese

Endive, Cheddar and Apple Salad with Almond Oil Dressing   78

Gruyère, Belgian Endive and Tagliatelle Salad with Creamy Chive Dressing   80

Rustic Greek Salad   82

English Spinach, Radicchio, Avocado and Blue Cheese Salad with Walnut Vinaigrette   84

Arugula and Parmesan Salad with Walnut Oil Dressing   86

Baked Goat Cheese Salad with Balsamic Vinaigrette   88

Fruit

Beet and Orange Salad   90

Avocado, Fennel and Orange Salad with Balsamic Vinaigrette   92

Carrot, Peanut and Raisin Salad with Cumin Dressing   94

Practicalities

sherry vinegar

walnut oil

olive oil

balsamic vinegar

macadamia
nut oil

hazelnut oil

tarragon vinegar

Oils & Vinegars

raspberry vinegar

basil oil

white wine vinegar

extra virgin
olive oil

red wine
vinegar

Tuna and Citrus Salad

10 oz (315 g) red-skinned potatoes
1 tablespoon olive oil
7 oz (220 g) fresh tuna fillet
2 large oranges
1 small grapefruit
1 red onion, sliced into rings
½ cup (3 oz/90 g) green olives
¼ cup (¼ oz/7.5 g) loosely packed
  fresh coriander (cilantro) leaves

Dressing:
2 tablespoons fresh lime juice
2 tablespoons fresh orange juice
1 tablespoon red wine vinegar
2 tablespoons extra virgin olive oil
1 small red chili, seeded and finely
  chopped

Cook the potatoes whole, with their skins on, in boiling salted water until tender, about 20 minutes. Drain and let cool.

Heat the olive oil in a small frying pan and cook the tuna until it is just cooked through, 3–5 minutes on each side, according to taste. Drain on paper towels and set aside to cool.

Peel the oranges and grapefruit. Remove all pith and cut into segments.

Dressing: Combine all the dressing ingredients in a small bowl and whisk together thoroughly.

Cut the cooled potatoes into bite-size pieces. Break the tuna into small chunks.

Combine all the salad ingredients in a large bowl and pour on the dressing. Carefully toss to coat.

Serves 4 as an appetizer
Preparation/Cooking Time: 30 minutes

14

Warm Mussel Salad with Red Bell Pepper and Caper Dressing

Dressing:

1 red bell pepper (capsicum),
  roasted, peeled and diced
1 large tomato, peeled, seeded and
  diced
1 small red onion, diced
2 tablespoons tiny capers, drained
¼ cup (2 fl oz/60 ml) extra virgin
  olive oil
1 tablespoon balsamic vinegar
salt and black pepper

4 lb (2 kg) mussels
1 cup (8 fl oz/250 ml) dry white
  wine
2 cloves garlic, crushed

*D**ressing:** Combine all of the dressing ingredients in a small bowl and mix thoroughly. Set aside for at least 30 minutes, to allow the flavors to develop.

Clean the mussels thoroughly by scrubbing them with a brush or scourer. Remove their beards.

Heat the wine and garlic in a large nonreactive saucepan. Add the mussels, cover and cook for about 5 minutes, or until the mussels open. Drain the mussels and discard any that do not open.

Remove the empty half of each mussel shell. Arrange the full shell halves on a serving platter. Spoon a little dressing into each.

Serve while the mussels are still warm, with crusty bread.

Serves 6 as a main course
Preparation/Cooking Time: 30 minutes

Caesar Salad

1 head French lettuce or
   5 oz (155 g) baby spinach leaves
1 small head cos lettuce
1 clove garlic, halved
5 tablespoons olive oil
¾ cup (¾ oz/20 g) white bread
   cubes
1 can (1½ oz/45 g) anchovies,
   drained
2 eggs
½ cup (1¾ oz/50 g) Parmesan
   cheese shavings

Dressing:

2 tablespoons lemon juice
5 tablespoons olive oil
freshly ground black pepper

Wash the lettuce leaves carefully and set aside. Heat the olive oil in a frying pan over medium heat, add the garlic and the bread cubes and cook until golden on all sides. Drain on kitchen paper and discard the garlic.

Dressing: Whisk the lemon juice, olive oil and pepper together in a small bowl until well blended.

Halve the anchovies lengthwise. Boil the eggs for 1 minute.

While the eggs are boiling, place the lettuce leaves in a large serving bowl, pour the dressing over the leaves and toss to coat thoroughly.

Break the eggs into the salad and mix again thoroughly.

Scatter the salad with the anchovies, bread croutons and Parmesan. Toss again gently and serve immediately.

Serves 4 as an appetizer
Preparation Time: 25 minutes

Smoked Salmon, Potato, and Fennel Salad with Dill and Mustard Vinaigrette

2 medium fennel bulbs
3 large waxy potatoes
5 oz (155 g) smoked salmon,
   thinly sliced

Dressing:
6 tablespoons olive oil
juice of 1 lemon
1 teaspoon sherry vinegar
1 teaspoon Dijon mustard
1 teaspoon coarse mustard
freshly ground black pepper
1 tablespoon finely chopped dill
1 generous pinch brown sugar

Halve the fennel bulbs and remove the cores. Cook the fennel in boiling salted water until tender, about 15 minutes. Add a few drops of vinegar to the water to prevent the fennel discoloring.

Cook the potatoes whole with the skins intact, in boiling salted water until just tender, about 20 minutes. Set the vegetables aside to cool.

Slice the fennel into thin wedges. Cut the potatoes into ½-inch (1 cm) slices.

Dressing: Combine all of the ingredients in a small bowl and whisk until well combined.

Arrange the fennel, potato and smoked salmon on a serving platter. Pour the dressing evenly over the ingredients.

Serve at room temperature.

Serves 4–6 as an appetizer
Preparation/Cooking Time: 30 minutes

Smoked Trout and Avocado Croûton Salad

1 baguette or French bread stick,
    cut into ½ inch (1.5 cm) slices
olive oil
1 whole smoked trout (about
    8 oz/250 g)
1 large ripe avocado
lemon wedges, for garnish
dill sprigs, for garnish

Dressing:
½ cup (4 fl oz/125 ml) sour cream
½ cup (4 fl oz/125 ml)
    mayonnaise
¼ cup (2 oz/60 g) finely chopped
    fresh dill
1 tablespoon drained tiny capers
2 tablespoons fresh lemon juice

Preheat oven to 375°F (190°C/Gas 5).
Arrange the bread slices on a baking sheet. Brush each slice with olive oil. Bake, turning once, until light golden on both sides, about 15 minutes. Remove from the oven and set aside to cool.

Meanwhile, using a sharp knife, carefully remove the skin and bones from the smoked trout. Cut the trout fillets into small pieces.

Peel, pit and slice the avocado.

Dressing: Combine all the dressing ingredients in a bowl and mix thoroughly. Stir in the avocado and smoked trout.

Top each croûton with some of the mixture and arrange on a serving platter. Garnish with lemon wedges and dill sprigs.

Serves 4 as an hors d'oeuvre
Preparation/Cooking Time: 30 minutes

Warm Thai Chicken Salad

Chicken and Marinade:

6 single, skinless, boneless chicken
  fillets (about 1¼ lbs/600 g)
¼ cup (2 fl oz/60 ml) fresh lemon
  juice
¼ teaspoon salt
2 cloves garlic, crushed
1 tablespoon brown sugar
2 tablespoons finely chopped fresh
  coriander (cilantro)

Dressing:

1 small red chili, finely chopped
1 clove garlic, finely chopped
3 tablespoons extra virgin olive oil
1 tablespoon balsamic vinegar
juice of 2 limes
1 teaspoon sweet chili sauce

1 bunch (14 oz/440 g) mizuna
1 red bell pepper (capsicum), seeds
  and membrane removed and
  cut into julienne
2 carrots, cut into julienne
1 cucumber, cut into julienne
6 green (spring) onions, sliced
1 cup (1 oz/30 g) loosely packed
  fresh coriander (cilantro) sprigs
1 cup (1 oz/30 g) shredded purple
  basil
3 tablespoons Oriental sesame oil
3 tablespoons toasted sesame seeds

Flatten the chicken fillets slightly and cut each lengthwise into 4 strips. Combine all of the marinade ingredients in a shallow ceramic bowl and mix well. Add the chicken and toss to coat. Set aside, covered in plastic wrap in the refrigerator overnight, or at room temperature for several hours.

Dressing: Combine all the dressing ingredients in a small bowl and whisk until well combined.

Combine the mizuna, red bell pepper (capsicum), carrot, cucumber, green (spring) onions and herbs on 6 individual serving plates.

Heat the sesame oil in a wok or frying pan until smoking. Stir-fry the chicken until cooked through, about 3 minutes. Divide the chicken among the serving plates. Drizzle on the dressing and sprinkle with the toasted sesame seeds.

Serve immediately, while the chicken is still warm.

Serves 6 as an appetizer or light lunch
Preparation/Cooking Time: 30 minutes
Marinating Time: Several hours or overnight in refrigerator

Chicken Gado Gado

1 chicken (3 lbs/1.5 kg), cooked,
  bones removed and meat cut
  into bite-size pieces
½ Chinese cabbage, shredded
13 oz (410 g) small new potatoes,
  cooked until tender and cooled
1 small cucumber, cut into
  julienne
6½ oz (200 g) carrots, peeled and
  cut into julienne
1½ cups (5 oz/155 g) bean
  sprouts, rinsed and drained
¾ cup (1¾ oz/50 g) sliced shallots
¼ cup (¼ oz/7.5 g) coriander
  (cilantro) sprigs, for garnish

Dressing:

1 tablespoon olive oil
1 onion, finely chopped
1 clove garlic, crushed
1 tablespoon curry powder
1 tablespoon brown sugar
1 tablespoon soy sauce
juice ½ lemon
2 teaspoons white wine vinegar
1 teaspoon hot chili sauce
¼ cup (2 fl oz/60 ml) dry sherry
½ cup (4 oz/125 g) crunchy
  peanut butter
1 cup (8 fl oz/250 ml) coconut
  milk

Arrange the vegetables in layers on a large serving platter in the order in which they are listed. Top with the chicken. Refrigerate the platter until needed.

Dressing: Heat the oil in a pan over medium heat. Add the onion and garlic and cook for a few minutes until the onion is soft. Add all of the remaining dressing ingredients, except the peanut butter and coconut milk. Simmer over low heat for 5 minutes.

Add the peanut butter and coconut milk and stir until well combined. Simmer over low heat for about 3 minutes, or until the sauce thickens slightly. Cover the surface of the sauce with plastic wrap and allow to cool to room temperature.

Just before serving, spoon the sauce over the assembled salad and garnish with the coriander (cilantro) sprigs.

Serves 6 as a main course
Preparation/Cooking Time: 45 minutes

Chicken, Avocado and Mango Salad with Creamy Curry and Macadamia Dressing

Dressing:

3 tablespoons olive oil

1 onion, finely chopped

2 teaspoons curry powder

1 tablespoon apricot jelly or jam

1 tablespoon mango chutney

¼ cup (1 oz/30 g) unsalted macadamia nuts

2 tablespoons raspberry vinegar

½ cup (4 fl oz/125 ml) mayonnaise

¼ cup (2 fl oz/60 ml) light (single) cream

4 skinless, boneless, single chicken breasts, poached

1 bunch (3½ oz/100 g) arugula (rocket), washed and stemmed

2 large mangoes, peeled, pitted and sliced

2 large avocados, peeled, pitted and sliced

1 bunch fresh chives, cut into 2 inch (5 cm) lengths, for garnish

*D*ressing: Heat 1 tablespoon of the oil over medium heat in a small saucepan. Add the onion and cook until translucent. Add the curry powder and cook, stirring, for 1 minute. Remove from the heat and stir in the apricot jelly or jam and mango chutney, mixing well. Set aside until cool.

In a blender or food processor, process the macadamia nuts briefly until chopped, add the remaining oil and the vinegar and process until well combined.

Add the nut mixture to the cooled onion mixture. Stir in the mayonnaise and cream. Mix well.

Slice the cooked chicken breasts lengthwise into 5 or 6 strips. Combine the arugula (rocket), chicken, mango and avocado on individual serving dishes. Spoon some of the dressing on to each serving.

Garnish with the chives and serve immediately.

Serves 4
Preparation Time: 30 minutes

Goat Cheese, Pancetta and Asparagus Salad with Hazelnut Vinaigrette

3½ oz (100 g) pancetta, thinly
  sliced
2 bunches (9 oz/280 g) fresh
  asparagus
1 tablespoon hazelnut oil
3 tablespoons hazelnuts, skins
  removed
1 head (3½ oz/100 g) butter
  lettuce, washed and torn
1 head (3½ oz/100 g) green
  oakleaf lettuce, washed and torn
5 oz (155 g) goat cheese, sliced or
  crumbled

Dressing:
2 tablespoons hazelnut oil
1 tablespoon white wine vinegar
1 tablespoon light olive oil

Broil (grill) the pancetta slices until crisp. Drain on paper towels and break into pieces.

Halve the asparagus spears lengthwise and blanch in boiling salted water until just tender. Run under cold water. Drain.

Heat the hazelnut oil in a small frying pan. Toss the hazelnuts in the oil and toast until golden.

Dressing: Combine all of the dressing ingredients in a small bowl. Whisk until thoroughly combined.

Combine the lettuces, goat cheese, pancetta, asparagus and hazelnuts on individual plates. Drizzle on the dressing and serve immediately.

Serves 4 as an appetizer or light lunch
Preparation/Cooking Time: 20 minutes

Baked Red Bell Pepper and Salami Salad

3 red bell peppers (capsicums)
3 red onions
2 cloves garlic
¼ cup (2 fl oz/60 ml) olive oil
4 oz (125 g) spicy Italian salami, roughly chopped
½ jar (4½ oz/140 g) artichoke hearts, drained and halved
⅓ cup (3½ oz/100 g) small black olives
2 teaspoons dried oregano
1 tablespoon balsamic vinegar

Halve the bell peppers (capsicums) and remove the seeds and membranes. Cut each half into 4 pieces. Peel the onions and cut each into eighths. Peel and chop the garlic and combine with the olive oil.

Preheat oven to 400°F (200°C/Gas 6).

Arrange the pepper slices and onions in a shallow baking dish. Pour on the garlic oil. Bake for 20 minutes.

Remove the baking dish from the oven and stir the peppers and onions gently. Add the salami, artichokes, olives and oregano. Return to the oven for 15 minutes. Remove from oven and drizzle with the balsamic vinegar.

Serve warm, or at room temperature, with crusty bread.

Serves 6 as an appetizer or accompaniment
Preparation/Cooking Time: 45 minutes

Rare Roast Beef Salad with Mustard Mayonnaise

Dressing:

⅓ cup (3½ fl oz/100 ml) olive oil
¼ cup (2 fl oz/60 ml) lemon juice
2 tablespoons finely chopped chives
1 tablespoon drained tiny capers
1 tablespoon finely chopped
   sun-dried bell pepper
   (capsicum)
salt and freshly ground black
   pepper

Mustard Mayonnaise:

¼ cup (2 fl oz/60 ml) mayonnaise
1 tablespoon Dijon mustard
2 teaspoons Worcestershire sauce
a few drops of Tabasco sauce

3 lbs (1.5 kg) rare roast beef,
   sliced — allow 2 large slices per
   person
6 oz (185 g) cherry tomatoes,
   halved
1 head (3½ oz/100 g) radicchio,
   washed and torn
1 bunch (3½ oz/100 g) lamb's
   lettuce, washed and torn
1 jar (8 oz/250 g) artichoke
   hearts, halved
⅓ cup (2½ oz/75 g) tiny
   cornichons (tiny gherkins or
   dill pickles)

*D*ressing: Combine all of the dressing ingredients in a small bowl. Whisk together until well blended.

Mustard Mayonnaise: Combine all the mayonnaise ingredients in a small bowl. Stir until well blended.

Divide the remaining ingredients among 6 serving plates. Spoon the dressing over and place a tablespoon of mayonnaise in the center of each salad.

Serves 6 as a main course
Preparation Time: 30 minutes

Mixed Tomato, Prosciutto and Mozzarella Salad with Balsamic Vinaigrette

10 oz (315 g) plum tomatoes

5 oz (155 g) yellow tear-drop tomatoes

6 oz (185 g) cherry tomatoes

8 oz (250 g) small fresh mozzarella (bocconcini)

3½ oz (100 g) finely sliced prosciutto

1 cup (1 oz/30 g) basil leaves, torn if large

Dressing:

½ cup (4 fl oz/125 ml) extra virgin olive oil

2 tablespoons balsamic vinegar

salt and freshly ground black pepper

Slice the plum tomatoes into rounds. Halve the cherry and teardrop tomatoes. Slice the fresh mozzarella (bocconcini).

Dressing: Whisk together the olive oil and balsamic vinegar until well blended.

Arrange the salad ingredients on 4 individual serving plates. Drizzle some of the dressing over each salad.

Serve at room temperature.

Serves 4 as an appetizer or light lunch
Preparation Time: 15 minutes

Antipasto Salad Platter

Dressing:

½ cup (4 fl oz/125 ml) olive oil
2 tablespoons red wine vinegar
1 clove garlic, crushed
1 tablespoon finely chopped
  flat-leaf (continental) parsley
1 tablespoon capers, finely chopped
1 tablespoon finely chopped
  anchovy fillets
1 teaspoon tomato paste
½ teaspoon sugar
freshly ground pepper

2 lbs (1 kg) eggplant (aubergine),
  sliced into ½ inch (1 cm) rounds
salt
2 red bell peppers (capsicums)
1 yellow bell pepper (capsicums)
½ cup (2 oz/60 g) all-purpose
  (plain) flour
olive oil, for frying
13 oz (410 g) plum tomatoes,
  sliced lengthwise
10 oz (315 g) fresh mozzarella
  cheese (bocconcini), sliced

*D*ressing: Combine all of the dressing ingredients in a bowl. Whisk together thoroughly.

Place the eggplant (aubergine) slices in a colander. Lightly sprinkle with salt and set aside for 30 minutes.

Halve the bell peppers (capsicums) and remove the seeds and membrane. Place the bell pepper halves under a heated broiler (grill) and cook until the skins are blackened. Place the halves in a plastic bag and let cool. When they are cold enough to handle, peel off their skins and slice thinly. Set aside.

Rinse the eggplant slices and drain on kitchen paper. Dust the slices lightly with flour. Heat sufficient oil in a large frying pan to fry the eggplant slices in batches. Cook all of the slices until golden on both sides. As each slice is cooked, dip it in the prepared dressing and arrange around the serving platter.

Cook the tomato slices for a few seconds on each side in the same pan as the eggplant. Place the tomato slices on top of the eggplant. Top the tomato with the cheese slices. Spoon a little dressing over each mozzarella slice. Arrange the pepper slices in the center of the serving platter. Spoon on the remaining dressing. Let stand at room temperature for at least 1 hour before serving.

Serves 6–8 as an appetizer
Preparation Time: 30 minutes

Mixed Leaf Salad

12 oz (375 g) mixed lettuce leaves, such as mignonette, butter lettuce, green oakleaf, English spinach, arugula (rocket) and radicchio, washed and dried

Dressing:
¼ cup (2 fl oz/60 ml) extra virgin olive oil
1 tablespoon tarragon vinegar
1 teaspoon Dijon mustard
salt and freshly ground black pepper

Combine all of the salad leaves in a large serving bowl. Tear any larger leaves into manageable pieces.

Dressing: Combine all the dressing ingredients in a small bowl and whisk thoroughly.

Pour the dressing over the salad, toss thoroughly and serve immediately.

Serves 6 as an accompaniment
Preparation Time: 15 minutes

Spring Vegetable Salad with Tomato and Basil Salsa Dressing

Dressing:

13 oz (410 g) tomatoes, peeled,
   seeded and finely chopped

1 red onion, finely chopped

1 clove garlic, finely chopped

¼ cup (¼ oz/7.5 g) shredded fresh
   basil

½ teaspoon salt

freshly ground black pepper

2 tablespoons red wine vinegar

¼ cup (2 fl oz/60 ml) olive oil

4 oz (125 g) small green beans

1 bunch asparagus, trimmed

8 oz (250 g) small yellow squash

4 oz (125 g) baby corn

3½ oz (100 g) snow peas
   (mange tout)

1 yellow bell pepper (capsicum),
   halved, seeded and cut into
   thick strips

1 red bell pepper (capsicum),
   halved, seeded and cut into
   thick strips

12 baby carrots

2 tablespoons extra virgin olive oil

½ teaspoon salt

Dressing: Combine all of the dressing ingredients in a bowl and stir thoroughly. Set aside for 30 minutes to allow the flavor to develop.

Bring a large saucepan of water to a boil. Blanch each of the vegetables, one at a time, until just tender, 1–2 minutes each. Plunge each batch into ice water as it is removed from the hot water. Quarter the squash after blanching.

Combine the vegetables in a large bowl, add the extra virgin olive oil and salt and toss well.

Just before serving, pour the dressing over the salad and toss thoroughly.

Serves 6 as an accompaniment
Preparation/Cooking Time: 40 minutes

Warm Mixed Mushroom and Asparagus Salad

3½ oz (100 g) shiitake mushrooms
5 oz (155 g) button mushrooms
5 oz (155 g) oyster mushrooms
1 bunch (5 oz/155 g) asparagus
¼ cup (2 fl oz/60 ml) walnut oil
salt and freshly ground pepper
1 bunch (3½ oz/100 g) watercress,
   washed and dried
2 tablespoons raspberry vinegar

Clean the mushrooms with a damp cloth. Halve any large ones. Cut the asparagus into 2 inch (5 cm) lengths. Cook the asparagus in boiling salted water until just tender. Plunge into cold water. Drain.

Heat the walnut oil in a large wok or frying pan. Add the button and shiitake mushrooms and stir-fry for 2 minutes. Add the oyster mushrooms and stir-fry for 2 minutes. Add the asparagus and stir to combine. Season with salt and freshly ground black pepper.

Arrange the watercress on a serving plate. Pile the mushrooms and asparagus in the center.

Bring the raspberry vinegar to a boil in the pan used for the mushrooms. Pour the vinegar over the salad and serve.

Serves 6 as an appetizer or accompaniment
Preparation/Cooking Time: 20 minutes

Broiled Baby Eggplant Salad with Cumin, Coriander and Yogurt Dressing

11 oz (345 g) baby eggplants
  (aubergine)

5 oz (155 g) cherry tomatoes,
  halved

3 tablespoons olive oil

2 tablespoons red wine vinegar

1 clove garlic, crushed

salt and freshly ground black
  pepper

Dressing:

¼ cup (2 fl oz/60 ml) plain
  (natural) yogurt

¼ cup (2 fl oz/60 ml) sour cream

1 clove garlic

½ teaspoon freshly grated ginger

½ teaspoon salt

½ teaspoon ground cumin

1 tablespoon finely chopped fresh
  coriander (cilantro), plus sprigs
  of coriander (cilantro) for
  garnish

Preheat the broiler (grill).
   Using a sharp knife, slice the eggplant (aubergine) lengthwise into 3 or 4 segments, leaving the stem section intact. Fan out the slices. Brush with a little oil and broil (grill) on both sides until the eggplant is tender and slightly golden, 3–4 minutes.

Arrange the eggplants and the cherry tomatoes on a serving platter. Combine the olive oil, vinegar, garlic and salt and pepper in a small bowl. Whisk until well blended. Drizzle over the eggplants and tomatoes and allow to cool to room temperature.

Dressing: Combine all the dressing ingredients in a bowl and stir until thoroughly blended.

Just before serving, spoon some of the dressing over the eggplant and tomatoes. Garnish with fresh coriander (cilantro) sprigs.

Serves 4–6 as an accompaniment
Preparation/Cooking Time: 30 minutes

Baby Squash and Yellow Pepper Salad with Raspberry Vinaigrette

10 oz (315 g) mixed yellow and
   green baby squash
2 yellow bell peppers (capsicums)
a few sprigs chervil, to garnish

Dressing:
2 tablespoons raspberry vinegar
¼ cup (2 fl oz/60 ml) olive oil
2 teaspoons Dijon mustard
¼ teaspoon salt

Bring a large saucepan of salted water to a boil. Add the squash. When the water returns to full boil remove from the heat, drain the squash, and plunge them into cold water for 3 minutes. Drain and set aside.

Halve the peppers and remove the seeds and membrane. Place under the broiler (grill), and cook until their skins are blackened. Place the peppers in a plastic or paper bag and seal. Let cool. When cool, remove the skins from the peppers and cut them into thin strips.

Slice the squash finely and arrange in rows on a serving plate. Arrange strips of pepper between the rows.

Dressing: Combine all of the dressing ingredients in a small bowl. Whisk until well combined. Drizzle the dressing over the salad and set aside for at least 30 minutes to allow the flavors to develop before serving.

Serves 6 as an accompaniment
Preparation/Cooking Time: 25 minutes

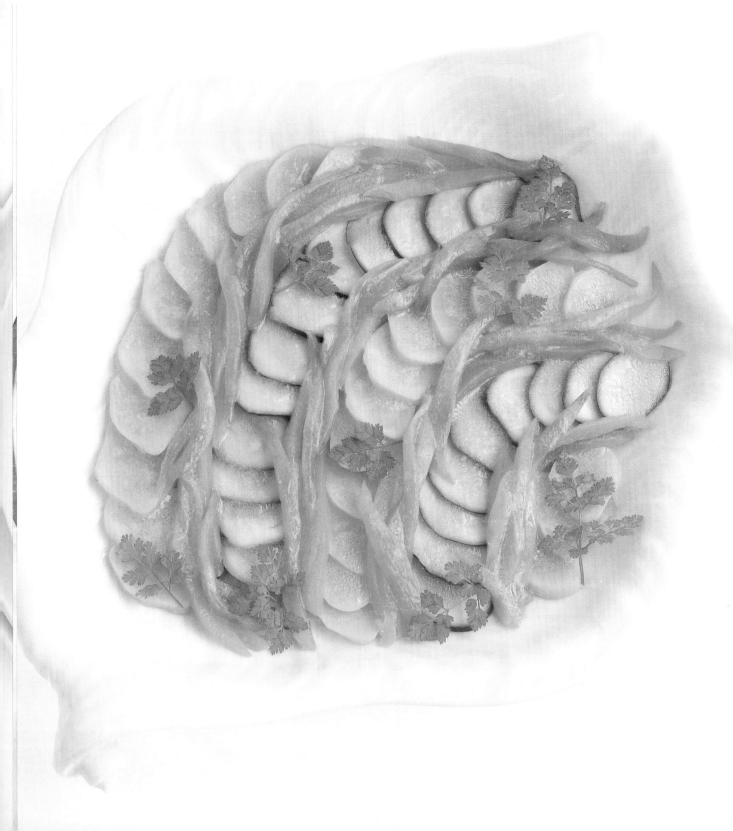

Roasted Tomato Salad

1¾ lbs (800 g) large tomatoes
1 bunch green (spring) onions
6 garlic cloves, peeled
5 tablespoons extra virgin olive oil
1 tablespoon fresh thyme leaves
freshly ground black pepper
1 tablespoon balsamic vinegar
1 tablespoon finely chopped flat-
   leaf (continental) parsley

Peel the tomatoes by covering them with boiling water for about 20 seconds then plunging them into cold water. Drain and carefully remove the skins. Halve the skinned tomatoes and squeeze out the seeds. Allow to drain for 30 minutes on a wire rack.

Preheat oven to 375°F (190°C/Gas 5).

Arrange the tomatoes, cut sides up, in a shallow baking dish. Halve the green (spring) onions and garlic cloves and add to the dish. Pour on the olive oil and scatter with the thyme and black pepper. Bake, uncovered, for 30 minutes. Remove from the oven and let cool.

When the tomatoes are cool enough to handle, arrange, cut side down, on a serving plate. Spoon on the green onions and garlic.

Whisk the balsamic vinegar into the oil that remains in the baking dish. Drizzle the mixture over the tomatoes and onions. Sprinkle with the parsley.

Serve warm or at room temperature. This salad makes a good accompaniment to roasted and broiled (grilled) meat.

Serves 4–6 as an accompaniment
Cooking/Preparation Time: 1 hour

Green Bean Salad with Roasted Macadamia Nuts and Macadamia Nut Oil Vinaigrette

*1 lb (500 g) thin green beans,
topped and tailed*

*3½ oz (100 g) macadamia nuts,
halved*

1 tablespoon macadamia nut oil

Dressing:

2 tablespoons olive oil

2 tablespoons macadamia nut oil

2 tablespoons white wine vinegar

1 clove garlic, crushed

juice of 1 lemon

*1 tablespoon finely chopped fresh
coriander*

*1 tablespoon finely chopped flat-
leaf (continental) parsley*

2 teaspoons clear honey

½ small fresh chili, seeds removed

Cook the beans in boiling salted water until barely tender, about 5 minutes. Refresh under cold water and drain.

Dressing: Combine all of the dressing ingredients in a small bowl. Whisk together until thoroughly blended.

While the beans are still warm, arrange them on a serving plate and pour over enough dressing to coat them thoroughly.

Toast the macadamia halves in the macadamia oil for a few minutes, until lightly toasted. Pour the nuts and oil over the beans.

Serve at room temperature.

Serves 6 as an accompaniment
Preparation/Cooking Time: 30 minutes

Herb and Potato Frittata Salad with Tomato and Onion Salsa

Tomato and Onion Salsa:

*2–3 large tomatoes (preferably
    vine ripened), skinned, seeded
    and finely chopped*
1 red onion, finely chopped
1 small clove garlic, crushed
½ teaspoon coarse (Kosher) salt
freshly ground black pepper
2 tablespoons red wine vinegar
*¼ cup (2 fl oz/60 ml) extra virgin
    olive oil*

*10 oz (315 g) potatoes, washed but
    not peeled*
6 large eggs
6½ oz (200 g) ricotta cheese
*1¾ oz (50 g) finely grated fresh
    Parmesan cheese*
*2 tablespoons finely chopped
    flat-leaf (continental) parsley*
*2 tablespoons finely chopped fresh
    basil*
salt and pepper
*1 bunch (4 oz/125 g) watercress,
    well washed, for serving*

*T*omato and Onion Salsa: Combine all the salsa ingredients in a bowl. Stir thoroughly and set aside for at least 30 minutes to allow the flavors to develop.

Cook the potatoes whole in boiling salted water until just tender. Cut into thin slices when cool enough to handle.

In a large mixing bowl, beat the eggs with the ricotta and Parmesan until the mixture is smooth. Stir in the parsley and basil. Season with salt and pepper to taste.

Preheat the broiler (grill). Oil a large frying pan, preferably a nonstick one. Spread half of the egg mixture over the bottom of the pan. Arrange the potato slices on top and spread with the remaining egg mixture. Cook over low to medium heat until the mixture is set, 10–15 minutes. Lightly brown the top of the frittata under broiler (grill) for 2–3 minutes. Slide the frittata on to a board or cutting surface. Let cool slightly.

Arrange the watercress over a serving platter. Cut the frittata into thin wedges and arrange over the watercress. Spoon on the Tomato and Onion Salsa and serve warm or at room temperature.

Serves 4 as a luncheon main course/6 as an appetizer
Preparation/Cooking Time: 45 minutes

Mixed Potato Salad with Mint Pesto Dressing

1 lb (500 g) waxy potatoes
1 lb (500 g) baby new potatoes
2 tablespoons pine nuts, toasted,
   for garnish

Dressing:
1 cup (1 oz/30 g) loosely packed
   mint leaves
2 tablespoons pine nuts
1 clove garlic, peeled
¼ teaspoon salt
¾ cup (1¾ oz/50 g) freshly grated
   Parmesan cheese
¼ cup (2 fl oz/60 ml) olive oil
½ cup (4 fl oz/125 ml) sour cream

Cook the potatoes in their skins in boiling salted water until tender, about 15–20 minutes. Drain, rinse and set aside to cool. When the potatoes are cool enough to handle, cut into bite-size chunks.

Dressing: Place the mint leaves, pine nuts, garlic, salt, Parmesan and oil in a blender or food processor. Process until the ingredients are well chopped and combined. Add the sour cream and mix to combine.

While the potatoes are still warm, pour the dressing over the potatoes and mix carefully until well coated.

Garnish the salad with the toasted pine nuts and serve at room temperature.

Serves 6 as an accompaniment
Preparation Time: 30 minutes

Couscous Tabbouleh

1½ cups (8 oz/250 g) instant
  couscous
1 cup (8 fl oz/250 ml) boiling
  water
3 large tomatoes, peeled, seeded
  and finely chopped
½ cup (1¾ oz/50 g) finely sliced
  green (spring) onions
¼ cup (¼ oz/7.5 g) finely chopped
  fresh mint leaves
1 cup (1 oz/60 g) finely chopped
  flat-leaf (continental) parsley

Dressing:
⅓ cup (2½ fl oz/75 ml) fresh
  lemon juice
2 tablespoons olive oil
1 teaspoon salt

Place the couscous in a large bowl. Pour on the boiling water and stir thoroughly. Set aside to allow the couscous to absorb the water and swell.

Dressing: Combine all the dressing ingredients in a small bowl and whisk thoroughly.

In a large serving bowl, combine the tomatoes, green (spring) onions, mint and parsley. Stir the couscous with a fork to separate the grains and break up any lumps. Add the couscous to the serving bowl and mix all the ingredients thoroughly. Pour on the dressing and mix again thoroughly.

Serve at room temperature, or chilled.

Serves 6 as an accompaniment
Preparation Time: 30 minutes

Wild Rice Salad with Orange Vinaigrette

¾ cup (4 oz/125 g) wild rice
½ cup (3½ oz/100 g) brown rice
¾ cup (4½ oz/140 g) raisins
½ cup (3 oz/90 g) chopped dried
   apricots
¼ cup (1½ oz/45 g) sesame seeds,
   toasted
½ cup (2½ oz/75 g) shelled
   pumpkin seeds
½ cup (2½ oz/75 g) pine nuts,
   toasted
½ cup (2½ oz/75 g) sunflower
   seeds, toasted

Dressing:
zest (rind) of 1 large orange
¼ cup (2 fl oz/60 ml) fresh orange
   juice
1 tablespoon lemon juice
1 teaspoon balsamic vinegar
½ teaspoon salt
3 tablespoons olive oil

Cook the wild rice and brown rice separately, according to the package directions. Soak the raisins and apricots separately in hot water for about 15 minutes.

Dressing: Combine all of the dressing ingredients in a small bowl and whisk until thoroughly blended.

In a large mixing bowl, combine all of the salad ingredients. Pour over the dressing and mix until thoroughly combined.

Serve at room temperature.

Serves 6 as an accompaniment
Preparation/Cooking Time: 1 hour 15 minutes

Jasmine Rice Salad

1 cup (5 oz/155 g) jasmine rice

¾ cup (1¾ oz/50 g) shredded
   coconut, toasted

½ cup (1½ oz/45 g) sliced green
   (spring) onions

½ red bell pepper (capsicum),
   diced

½ green bell pepper (capsicum),
   diced

½ cup (¾ oz/20 g) roughly
   chopped fresh coriander
   (cilantro)

1 small cucumber, diced

½ cup (1 oz/30 g) roughly chopped
   snow pea (mange tout) sprouts

Dressing:

juice of 1 lemon

3 tablespoons olive oil

½ small red chili, seeded and
   finely chopped

1 clove garlic, crushed

1 teaspoon clear honey

Cook the rice according to the package directions. Let cool. Combine the rice with all of the other salad ingredients and mix to combine.

Dressing: Combine all of the dressing ingredients in a small bowl. Whisk together thoroughly. Pour sufficient dressing over the salad to moisten the ingredients. Mix well.

Serve at room temperature.

Serves 6 as an accompaniment
Preparation Time: 30 minutes

Chick-pea Salad with Fresh Herb Vinaigrette

1 cup (6 oz/185 g) dried chick-peas (garbanzos)

2 medium tomatoes, skinned

3½ oz (100 g) black olives, pitted and sliced

1 purple (Spanish) onion, cut into fine rings

Fresh Herb Vinaigrette:

5 tablespoons olive oil

2 tablespoons red wine vinegar

1 tablespoon frsh lemon juice

1 clove garlic, crushed

1 tablespoon finely chopped flat-leaf (continental) parsley

1 tablespoon finely chopped fresh thyme

1 tablespoon finely chopped fresh rosemary

½ teaspoon sugar

salt and freshly ground black pepper

S oak the chick-peas (garbanzos) in cold water overnight. Drain. Cook in boiling salted water until tender, about 1 hour. Drain and refresh under cold water.

Halve the tomatoes, remove the seeds and chop finely. Combine the chick-peas, tomato, olives, and onion.

Dressing: Combine all of the dressing ingredients in a small bowl and whisk until thoroughly combined. Pour the dressing over the salad and mix until the ingredients are combined and well coated with the dressing.

Serve at room temperature as an accompaniment, or as part of an antipasto selection.

Serves 4–6 as an accompaniment
Preparation Time: 25 minutes (not including soaking and cooking chick-peas)

Endive, Cheddar and Apple Salad with Almond Oil Dressing

1 large green apple
1 large red apple
juice of 1 lemon
*2 endives, washed, trimmed and
    separated into spears*
1 cup (3½ oz/100 g) sliced celery
*4 oz (125 g) good-quality sharp
    cheddar cheese, thinly sliced*
*⅓ cup (1½ oz/45 g) sunflower
    seeds, toasted*
*⅓ cup (1½ oz/45 g) flaked
    almonds, toasted*

Dressing:
2 tablespoons olive oil
2 tablespoons almond oil
2 tablespoons tarragon vinegar
juice of ½ lemon

Cut the apples into quarters and remove the cores. Thinly slice and sprinkle with the lemon juice to prevent discoloration.

Arrange the endive, celery, apples and cheese on a large serving platter or in a bowl. Scatter with the sunflower seeds and almonds.

Dressing: Combine all the dressing ingredients in a small bowl and whisk until thoroughly blended. Pour the dressing over the salad and toss well.

Rye bread makes a good accompaniment to this salad.

Serves 4–6 as an accompaniment
Preparation Time: 20 minutes

Gruyère, Belgian Endive and Tagliatelle Salad with Creamy Chive Dressing

6½ oz (200 g) fine tagliatelle
  pasta
6½ oz (200 g) Belgian endive
  (witloof), washed and finely
  shredded
1 head (3½ oz/100 g) radicchio,
  washed and finely shredded
3 oz (90 g) Gruyère cheese
  shavings
½ large red bell pepper
  (capsicum), finely sliced

Dressing:
2 tablespoons lemon juice
3 tablespoons light olive oil
2 tablespoons light (single) cream
1 tablespoon mayonnaise
2 tablespoons snipped fresh chives
salt and pepper

Cook the tagliatelle in boiling salted water until *al dente*. Run under cold water and drain. Set aside until cold.

Combine all of the salad ingredients and the pasta in a large mixing bowl.

Dressing: Combine all of the dressing ingredients in a small bowl. Whisk together thoroughly. Pour the dressing over the salad and toss thoroughly.

Serve at room temperature.

Serves 4–6 as an appetizer or accompaniment
Preparation/Cooking Time: 30 minutes

Rustic Greek Salad

2 tablespoons olive oil
1 clove garlic, halved
2 cups (2 oz/60 g) ½ inch
    (1.5 cm) fresh white bread cubes
3½ oz (100 g) feta cheese, cubed
2 medium (8 oz/250 g) tomatoes,
    cut into small wedges
1 small cucumber, sliced
½ cup (1 oz/30 g) sliced shallots
½ large red bell pepper
    (capsicum), cut into chunks
½ cup (3½ oz/100 g) black olives
1 head (3½ oz/100 g) cos lettuce,
    washed and torn
2 tablespoons finely chopped
    flat-leaf (continental) parsley

Dressing:
3 tablespoons olive oil
1 tablespoon white wine vinegar
1 clove garlic, crushed
salt and freshly ground black
    pepper

Heat the olive oil in a frying pan. Add the garlic and the bread cubes and cook until golden on all sides. Drain on kitchen towels.

Combine the croûtons and all of the remaining salad ingredients in a large bowl.

Dressing: Combine all of the dressing ingredients in a small bowl. Whisk thoroughly until combined. Pour the dressing over the salad and toss gently but thoroughly.

Serve at room temperature.

Serves 4–6 as an accompaniment
Preparation/Cooking Time: 25 minutes

Arugula and Parmesan Salad with Walnut Oil Dressing

2 bunches arugula (rocket),
    washed and dried
½ cup (1¾ oz/50 g) Parmesan
    cheese shavings
freshly ground black pepper

Dressing:
¼ cup (2 fl oz/60 ml) walnut oil
1 tablespoon tarragon vinegar

Combine the arugula (rocket), Parmesan cheese and black pepper in a large serving bowl.

Dressing: Combine the dressing ingredients in a small bowl and whisk thoroughly.

Pour the dressing over the salad and toss thoroughly. Serve immediately.

Serves 6 as an accompaniment
Preparation Time: 15 minutes

Baked Goat Cheese Salad with Balsamic Vinaigrette

½ cup (4 fl oz/125 ml) milk

1 egg

4 disks (rounds) goat cheese (each about 3½ oz/100 g)

⅓ cup (1½ oz/45 g) all-purpose (plain) flour

1 cup (2¾ oz/80 g) white bread crumbs

2 tablespoons sweet (unsalted) butter

2 oz (60 g) arugula (rocket), washed and dried

1 small head radicchio, leaves torn into pieces

⅓ cup (1¾ oz/50 g) sun-dried tomatoes, sliced

5 oz (155 g) yellow pear (teardrop) tomatoes, halved

watercress, for garnish (optional)

Dressing:

½ cup (4 fl oz/125 ml) extra virgin olive oil

2 tablespoons balsamic vinegar

salt and freshly ground black pepper

Preheat oven to 350°F (180°C/Gas 4). Beat together the milk and the eggs in a small bowl. Coat each disk (round) of goat cheese by rolling first in the flour, then dipping in the egg mixture and then coating with the bread crumbs.

Melt the butter in a nonstick frying pan over medium heat. Cook the goat cheese disks for 2–3 minutes, or until lightly browned on both sides. Remove from heat and place the rounds on a baking sheet. Bake in preheated oven for 5 minutes, until the cheese is warmed through.

While the cheese is in the oven, arrange the salad leaves and tomatoes on individual serving plates.

Dressing: Combine all the dressing ingredients in a small bowl and whisk thoroughly.

Remove the goat cheese from the oven and place one round in the center of each salad. Drizzle with the dressing, garnish with the watercress, if desired, and serve immediately.

Serves 4 as an appetizer or light lunch
Preparation/Cooking Time: 30 minutes

Beet and Orange Salad

1 lb (500 g) fresh beets (beetroot)
2 large oranges
1 cup (1¾ oz/50 g) julienned
   green (spring) onions
¼ cup (1 oz/30 g) roughly chopped
   pistachio nuts

Dressing:

1 tablespoon walnut oil
3 tablespoons extra virgin olive oil
1 tablespoon balsamic vinegar
salt and pepper

Bring a large saucepan of salted water to a boil. Meanwhile, cut off the beet (beetroot) stems, leaving about 1 inch (2.5 cm) attached. Add the beets to the pan, reduce the heat, cover and simmer for 50–60 minutes, or until the beets are tender. Drain and run under cold water. Set aside to cool.

When the beets are cool enough to handle, peel and trim them. Cut into julienne. Peel the oranges, slice and cut into thin strips.

Dressing: Combine the dressing ingredients in a small bowl and whisk thoroughly.

In a serving bowl, arrange the beets, oranges and green (spring) onions in layers. Just prior to serving, pour on the dressing. Scatter with the chopped pistachios and serve.

Serves 6 as an accompaniment
Preparation/Cooking Time: 1 hour 10 minutes

Avocado, Fennel and Orange Salad with Balsamic Vinaigrette

1 small bulb of fennel

1 bunch arugula (rocket), washed and dried

2 medium avocados, peeled, pitted and sliced

2 oranges, all pith removed and cut into segments

1 red onion, cut into fine rings

1 cup (1¾ oz/50 g) snow pea (mange tout) sprouts, firmly packed

2 tablespoons pine nuts, toasted

Dressing:

1 clove garlic, crushed

½ cup (4 fl oz/125 ml) extra virgin olive oil

1 tablespoon balsamic vinegar

salt and freshly ground black pepper

Slice the base off the fennel bulb and discard. Remove any fronds and peel off the tough outer layer. Cut lengthwise in half, remove the core and discard. Slice the fennel thinly.

Dressing: Combine all the dressing ingredients in a small bowl and whisk together thoroughly.

Arrange the arugula (rocket) over a flat serving plate. Arrange the avocados, orange, fennel, onion and sprouts decoratively over the rocket. Sprinkle with the toasted pine nuts.

Drizzle with the dressing and serve immediately.

Serves 4–6 as an appetizer or accompaniment
Preparation Time: 25 minutes

Carrot, Peanut and Raisin Salad with Cumin Dressing

2 to 3 large (13 oz/410 g) carrots,
   cut into julienne
2 tablespoons sesame seeds, toasted
½ cup (2¾ oz/80 g) dry roasted
   peanuts, roughly chopped
½ cup (2½ oz/75 g) golden raisins
   (sultanas), chopped
2 tablespoons finely chopped fresh
   coriander (cilantro)

Dressing:
1 tablespoon olive oil
juice of 1 lemon
1 clove garlic, crushed
¼ teaspoon sugar
½ teaspoon ground cumin
salt and freshly ground black
   pepper

Combine all of the salad ingredients in a large bowl.
Dressing: Combine all of the dressing ingredients in a small bowl. Whisk thoroughly until combined. Pour the dressing over the salad and toss thoroughly.

Serve at room temperature. This salad makes a good accompaniment to a curry.

Serves 6 as an accompaniment
Preparation Time: 25 minutes

Smoked Salmon, Asparagus and Cantaloupe Salad with Red Bell Pepper Mayonnaise

Dressing:

1 red bell pepper (capsicum), roasted and peeled

⅓ cup (2½ fl oz/75 ml) mayonnaise

6½ oz (200 g) smoked salmon fillets, thinly sliced

1 bunch (11 oz/345 g) asparagus, blanched

1 cantaloupe (rockmelon), halved, seeded and scooped into balls

1 honeydew melon, halved, seeded and scooped into balls

dill sprigs, for garnish

This recipe is pictured on page 3.

***D**ressing:* In a food processor, process the roasted bell pepper (capsicum) until puréed. Stir the purée into the mayonnaise until thoroughly combined.

Spoon some of the dressing on to 4 individual plates. Arrange the salad ingredients on top, garnish with the dill and serve immediately.

Serves 4 as an appetizer or light lunch
Preparation Time: 30 minutes